THE BRIEF HISTORY OF
A DISREPUTABLE WOMAN

JANE HOLLAND

The Brief History of
a Disreputable Woman

BLOODAXE BOOKS

ISBN: 1 85224 417 8

First published 1997 by
Bloodaxe Books Ltd,
P.O. Box 1SN,
Newcastle upon Tyne NE99 1SN.

Bloodaxe Books Ltd acknowledges
the financial assistance of Northern Arts.

Cover printing by J. Thomson Colour Printers Ltd, Glasgow.

Printed in Great Britain by
Cromwell Press Ltd, Broughton Gifford, Melksham, Wiltshire.

For Yvonne, Katie and Becky

Acknowledgements

Acknowledgements are due to the editors of the following publications in which some of these poems, or versions of them, first appeared: *Blade, The Guardian, Iron, London Magazine, The Mail on Sunday, Making for Planet Alice (Bloodaxe Books, 1997), Oasis, PN Review, Poetry Review, Snooker Scene* and the *Times Literary Supplement.* 'Three Tests for Darwin Duke' was broadcast on *Kaleidoscope* (BBC Radio 4), and 'Love Me Not' on Radio Ulster.

I am grateful for an Eric Gregory Award from the Society of Authors and an Isle of Man Arts Council Travel Bursary, both awarded in 1996. I would also like to thank Maura Dooley and Brendan Kennelly for their encouragement.

Contents

11 Pulse
12 Cherchez la Femme
13 Sleepers
14 They Are a Tableau at the Kissing Gate
15 Bless This House
16 Hangover
17 Spin-Cycle
18 The Brief History of a Disreputable Woman
22 Baize Queens
24 The Bap-Butterers
25 Cheating
26 Flaw
27 The Newel-Post
28 Because
29 Sleep
30 The Wolf-Box
31 Ants
32 Night-Tree
33 Not a Love Poem
34 Three Tests for Darwin Duke
37 Loco
38 Green Waters
39 Love Me Not
40 Last Letter from Paris
41 Horoscope Dancing
42 Brighton Pilgrimage
46 Post-Sirenists
47 Wee Sleekit Tim'rous Beastie
48 The Translator
49 Misreading the Classics
52 Having read up on the subject
54 Bonfire
55 Century of Rain
56 Wavelength
57 Head for Heights
58 Original Sin
60 The Gift
61 Aphrodite Revisited

62   Forgetting to Remember

63   Canzoni

73   Song for the Living

78   Song for the Dying

'What have I earned for all that work,' I said,
'For all that I have done at my own charge?
The daily spite of this unmannerly town,
Where who has served the most is most defamed,
The reputation of his lifetime lost
Between the night and the morning...'

W.B. YEATS: 'The People'

Pulse

Why should I speak of motherhood?
I might as well describe breathing
and have done with it.

Why should I eulogise breasts?
Have you never seen one?

Is my cunt so deliciously unusual,
it deserves three stanzas now
and a lifetime of comment?

We are no different from men,
except that a rapid pulse
beats hard at cunt and breast,

where a small white hand
can be seen emerging
or clutching a fold of skin
like a love-letter, suckling.

I am not a woman poet.
I am a woman and a poet.
The difference is in the eyes.

Cherchez la Femme

There is rain
on the windows when I am born
no cries
into a cold November.
The midwife is Caribbean,
complaining of these British winters
even as I slide
into her arms.

Rain becomes my season.
I walk out under the dark clouds
like a missionary,
preaching the world of the wet.
I kneel on the earth,
put my face to the dampness
like a child
hidden in her mother's skirt.

Later, unable to wear lace,
I finger photographs
of beautiful women.
Run my hands along lapels,
loving the coarseness of a country tweed,
the brisk crease of a man's shirt.
I sit apart,
smoke French cigarettes,
unfiltered,

my room dark with desire.
Each night, it falls at my window
like sharp insistent rain.
My desire is insatiable.
It has many names.
Watching through streaked glass,
I know none of them.

Sleepers

Under the green skirt of the sycamore
we kissed, or loved in other ways.
We asked no questions, had no need.

The sky was china-blue, like all the summers
of our youth: cloudless, undemanding.
We came to love too easily those days,

not thunder-struck, or lightning-shot,
but something underwritten, guaranteed.
A contract we agreed indulgently

like pouring double cream on strawberries,
or shutting out the night-cry with the cat
as if some simple act could silence it.

That piercing cat-call should have woken us,
but we walked those years like sleepers do,
sensing blindly where our feet should fall.

The shanty house we built out on the branch:
wild blossom thrown like rice at other kids,
your father's voice, late sunlight on a pool;

these carried us through years of innocence
and into times that took us by surprise,
too rough to measure on our little scale.

They Are a Tableau at the Kissing-Gate

Maids of honour, bridegroom, bride,
the best man in a grey silk suit,
a flash to catch them in the arching
stone, confettied by a sudden gust –
an apple tree in full white spread
beyond the reach of bone and dust.

I am the driver in a passing car:
the wedding-dress a cloud of lace.
A small hand clutching at a skirt,
some nervous bridesmaid, eight
or maybe nine years old, has seen
the blossom fall, has closed her eyes –

her head falls back into the scent,
the soundless whirr and whirl of earth-
bound petals, like sycamore seeds
on a current of air, silent helicopters
bringing light – a wedding-gift
the bride will brush away, unconsciously.

This is the bell above the kissing-gate,
the wind shaking the apple bark,
the sudden drift of blossom into light:
where they step out together arm in arm,
the blossom will still fall, unstoppable –
a drift of change across a changeless time.

Bless This House

You stand there in the dim light
from the patio, just checking
and rechecking your check list.

I'm perched on the rough edge
of a tea-chest, gently unscrewing
the last light bulb as ordered,

leaving the bare cord to swing.
I wipe the dust from my fingers
and hear you go out of the house,

your empty steps echoing. I run
a slow hand round the fixtures.
The kitchen stares coldly back.

The new place is bigger than this.
Already our old stuff is spilling
out of cedar closets, cluttering

hallways and the bare-board floors.
Beside the French windows, I pause
to watch the apple tree bend slowly

in the wind, tangled rope-swing rotten.
'We'll be happy here,' you said.
That salt over your left shoulder

was purely a reflex action, love.

Hangover

(for Judy and David)

Magnolia bleeds gently
into the silence,
an open cup, opened up
to a white morning.

When the stench
in the sickroom thickens
to a dull fog,
the magnolia cup

tips wax petals
like bathers
into a hot sun, melting.
The stone step says nothing.

Your red MX clatters
into the silence, then stills,
letting the dark hood
click down through the stages.

The magnolia too
listens without meaning
to the soft whirr
of an engine, defending.

Spin-Cycle

You've been blackberrying again.
I take your blouse
and watch it turn

through the white suds
in the drum, rinse-hold,
spinning slowly through the cycle.

I hear you up above,
bouncing on the bed
to reach the oval mirror,

see the purple stains
around your mouth and chin,
the blackness under nails

and in your hair.
Soon, like your swan-necked sister,
you will not have to stretch

on tiptoe for the sink
or grip the rail
when coming down the stairs.

You say 'when'.
I do not have the answers.
Just the slow loop

of your blouse
growing heavy with water,
as one cycle ends
and waits upon another.

The Brief History of a Disreputable Woman

It starts here as a table
in a back room. A busy pub,
a sideways look. The girls all

cheering when I drop the black.
A moment in between the kids,
a breath of silence slow

but true, across a table
in a small back room:
saying yes for once, not no.

Like Lazarus, I walk
from sleep, still stripping
off the winding sheet,

and take a cue from the rack
at the back of the club,
into the darkness

like a somnambulant.
Here hatred
breeds in corners at my step

and whispers
fall like evening
through these hanging lamps,

the gold-fringed shades.
This cloth is a lawn
to lay my head on, listening

to the beat of earth. They stare
from bar-stools, stalk me.
The men close ranks:

their shields reflect
like mirrors
as I clear the slate.

I am unwelcome here.
The door is there, they say,
and take the time to show me out.

But I am back again tomorrow.
Sliding the new cue
like a blade from its sheath,

polishing balls
until reflections turn to circles
in their goldfish eyes.

They cannot shut me out.
I have a right, a claim to stake
across this battlefield,

this bed of slate.
Their smiles are baited,
locked in place

until the silence is a war
that I seek out –
no choice of arms:

I fight left-handed on their ground.
I play the men.
I lose

and then I lose again.
I learn to stroke the ball away,
to catch the centre when I can,

find that timing
when the going's sweet,
the baize is running like a race-horse

and the bets are down.
To take the risks
and never cheat.

I watch the best:
mesmerised as
body moves to wrist,

wrist falls to hand,
this silent discipline
of heart and mind.

I hammer home
each lesson
like a goldsmith,

working a delicate grip
into the hit,
the pendulum arm true

as a perfect right-angle
when the cue
goes through.

I start to win:
short sharp burst
of pure adrenalin.

I learn to dodge
these empty shafts of sunlight
in the club, the arrows

when a woman
who walks alone
through rows

and rows of tables
dares to call them home.
Then others come.

They walk in,
taking the dust-covers
from the baize

with an awkward hand,
learning the touch of the cloth,
the deep furrow

left by a still hand,
fingers spread like a starfish.
First we are two,

then three, then four.
I pull them in from businesses,
supermarket queues,

from raising kids, from streets,
from empty doorways,
darkened rooms.

Together,
we are stronger.
We take a name for ourselves

and make it ring.
We play
each competition

in the spirit of the game –
a name engraved
in silver on a cup.

Retribution comes
not through games on baize
but in changing truths to fit

the end, till nothing's
what it seems. In their lies,
I recognise revenge.

I'll not give them what they want –
a public apology.
This ban is straight and true.

What started as a sideways look
will run for life,
for disrepute.

Baize Queens

We know this is not life.
Life does not have these corners
cut to pockets on the baize.

We take it oh so seriously though.
We fight to put the black away.
This is not life

but it's as near as dammit
when the green's running smooth
as silk and you're thirty points ahead.

This is not big money, no.
Not for women anyhow,
but still we do it all for love

or so they like to tell us.
This is our battleground.
Like Amazons,

we'd cut our tits off just to win.
We bitch in bathrooms
at the interval

and have our fill
of men who pat our heads
and pat our bums

and show us how to screw
or hold the cue
and ram it up their arses

if we're lucky.
Still, it's just a game.
Always shake her hand

and never cheat. Well played.
That last black really wiped its feet.
Give me a broom

I'll clear the bloody table.
This may not be life
but it's as near as dammit, girls.

The Bap-Butterers

(Glen Helen Lodge, TT Week)

Five to a table,
they are ten pairs of hands
working in unison.

Each bap is split
to a butterfly,
oiled like a woman in the sun.

Rosemary is cheese,
Miles ham –
the rest are turkey breast.

Even the radio dial
is floured,
pouring hip-hop out

into the slicing,
spreading
and the pressing

like a hot-house disco
where heat
pumps out the kitchen beat,

moving like a samba,
a cha–cha,
a long snake undulating,

a Mexican wave,
all hands on deck
and a fair bap following.

Cheating

Creeping out at night is an art form.
Shoes in hand, missing the loose stair,
slipping an oiled key through the lock
with the gentlest of turns: child's play.
Then out into the dark, the cool stars.

Dropping the handbrake: free-wheeling slowly
down the hill, engine bursting into life
past the first corner and onto the straight.
Then there's the time check: just long enough
to get out, get off and get back.

The trick is knowing when not to chance it.
Insomnia. The glass of water at three a.m.
A late film. But most times he's sleeping
like a baby, so that the light tread past
his bed goes unnoticed and unknown.

Some nights I don't bother. Just lie there
and watch the bright strip of headlights
move slowly over the dark ceiling.
Listen to the sound of his breathing.
Sometimes it feels good to be good.

Flaw

This hairline fracture in my face
falls short of early trends,
an undevelopment that means
the opposite of their intent.

What hope was there for us,
brought up on *how it was*
and *how it's meant to be*,
a crack across the times as wide

as love itself, this sediment
ingrained around the bath,
a grime that leaves its stain
on everyone and everything.

The guilt of never being them
condemns us to this albatross,
a war we never waged, a price
we've paid for what they lost.

This time it's ours, our turn
to make the same mistakes,
to fill our children's heads
with hope, to give them just

enough to hang themselves.

The Newel-Post

Where her passing hand had always touched.
Where feet of generations pause
for wood, whitewashed, under their fingers.

Up there, below the eaves, brushing stiffly
against shadows at the top of the stairs,
there is a music in the creaking boards.

It comes like rain, tapping out its rhythm
in darkness, a blind man with a stick.
I wait for the inevitable hand, welcome it.

Once, she was there for a whole evening,
sitting on her own with the hall-light off.
I think I might have heard her crying

but it could just have been the cat,
lashing a black tail around my frame.
She played that message again and again.

At night, I am a magnet for moonlight.
I count myself to the tick of the clock.
Upstairs, somebody wakes, coughs softly.

I will keep awake for them: alert
to the brisk feet of whistling milkmen,
the newspaper thud, a slither of post.

She never seems to see me, though I watch her
sometimes when she leaves the door ajar,
the kettle on, my painted surface steaming.

I recognise her by her changing tread.
I am that point along the passageway
where flesh and spirit tremble into wood.

Because

Is it because I bend
or seem to bend, or mend each bridge
before I've dreamt of burning it?

Is it because this eye has closed
or seems to close, or knows without
the clarity of sight what might not be?

Is it because I clamp the hate
or seem to clamp the hate, or wait
till I am asked for love?

Is it because we all agree,
or seemingly agree, or seem to see
the same light in the sky?

Is it because I cry,
or seem to cry, that I appear to be
as weightless as a cabbage-fly?

Is it because this tongue,
this silent dying tongue,
has never said or seemed to say *it's wrong*?

Sleep

The green arch of the bridge says *sleep*
The low slope of the field says *sleep*
The vole, lowering its head in the hedgerow, says *sleep*

The evening smoke says *sleep*
The white wall and the white fence say *sleep*
The canal, turning and wending, says *sleep*

The grim army of pylons says *sleep*
The dream of the cows, dreaming, says *sleep*
The leaf, midway between green and gold, says *sleep*

The flat shock of the horizon says *sleep*
The red tiles of the station say *sleep*
The fierce heart, unbending, says *sleep*

and *sleep* again.

But the coiled snake of the soul, hissing,
retreating, slipping its leash
and beating its tail at the door of the heart
says *wake, wake* and *the fall is forever.*

The Wolf-Box

My tongue
has its own blackness,
like the rough space in the heart of a fox
trapped too long within walls.

You conjured these claws,
invited them in
to the plunge of a shoulder.
Go shut the doors –

the wind has found this place –
we are no longer safe from wolves.
My face is white as their teeth
and bared to the bone.

Control, like beauty,
is skin-deep; it
unpeels itself, recoils
from the endless battery on the senses.

I cannot sleep tonight,
but watch the television flicker,
waiting for something
to be violent at.

Ants

The window is a sightless eye-socket
blasted like a war-zone crater in the wall,
and this bed is too narrow, I can hardly
turn on my side to read or drink water.
Outside, I can hear the black tread
of ants, they follow me everywhere,

even to the bathroom where they crawl
over my slack pale skin with their bodies
bristling with antennae like television aerials,
their small shiny heads nodding, glistening.
I can hear them whispering about me.
They file out, hold meetings, delegate.

The curtains are lime green: I have been
studying them for weeks now, I know
every stain, every tiny discolouration
of the cloth. Even the ants seem to have
realised; they always avoid them, taking
the longer route down the white wall.

I will be leaving here any day now.
They came round yesterday evening,
but the black ants were everywhere –
I could hardly hear a word that was said,
with all the itching, the drag and pinch
of their needles piercing my skin.

Night-Tree

Stupid mouth and stupid mind,
too dense with memory,
a night-tree clotted with the black of wings,
these gristled teeth, a tongue
that hardens with misuse.

The glass has found my empty shadow
in the hall, it slides
across the floor, the cracking wall.
The night-tree fades.
Its echoes fall and fight.

I find another word for glittering.
It only leads me back to light.
Too many shades where darkness
has just one. I'm indistinct
as silence on a starless night.

What makes me smoke and smoke?
I am recalcitrant.
I kick my heels against the past.
The mirror will not break.
It ghosts me like a window draft.

I came to life
as blank and cold as hell.
I am in quarantine.
Drugged up, morphined,
I am not well. I am not well.

The night-tree thickens with the night.
I sicken with the scent of blood.
Useless mouth: raw meat, deformed,
I'm dead from the inside out.
My tongue lolls, a barren seed.

Not a Love Poem

Sing me a love-song that has nothing to do with love.
Write me a line that cuts straight to the bone.

Show me a heart bent back like a blade,
white as a knuckle in the heat and the hate of despair.

Throw me your silence like the slow arc of a curve-ball.
Avoid my eyes, they are terrible as truth.

Three Tests for Darwin Duke

I

When I was a kid, still in short trousers,
peeping through windows
to see the colour of my neighbour's underwear,
I wanted to be a fireman
and chase that red-faced bell-borne fire-truck
straight through the centre of town
like a hero, hell-spawned and almost eaten alive
by the wicked white tongue of a fire too hot for the hose,
shattering windows with the blunt edge of an axe,
rescuing women in their buttoned nightclothes,
hair loose and lightly singed on their shoulders
who were always extremely grateful afterwards.

But the Duke became a caretaker instead
before they kicked me out
for setting the alarm off once a week
so I could hang out the window
and watch those engines screaming in,
sirens blaring in the heat of the day
and those firemen riding its hot red sides
like the Horsemen of the Apocalypse.
Then I'd pull out of the crowd
some sweat-faced girl in pigtails
and tell her it was safest in the boiler room
where pipes fan down their long black tentacles
dripping with oil and full of the reek of darkness
and I'd feel her up against the wall
until she laughed, when I'd drop her back
by her class and go home to my own woman
who always smells like a side of bacon
and who often laughs too, but for a different reason.
I guess I never really wanted to be a fireman.

II

This is the Duke on the line again.
I'm spinning a yarn – are you following?
What's a boy to do with a mother like mine,
a woman who never ran away to join a circus in her life,
although she wanted to
once or twice, but never spoke it aloud
in case I took her at her word:
saw her, sequinned, hanging from a rope
in that billowing canvas,
the death-wish of a golden mane
bunched like a fistful of corn beneath her,
two steps back from the raised chair
of a tamer, but herself untamed
in that great tide of people roaring
the foot-stamp ring of their clapping,
yet she blinked that thought at me
three times under her eyelids,
on her knees in the dust of the yard, praying
or just scrubbing the doorstep.
She baked it into her meat and potato pies
and the rise of her home-made bread, like a secret
written in flour on her shining forehead,
bright and coarse from the heat of the oven
or the long slow slop of water on a scrubbing-board.
'Darwin,' she would say,
although my father christened me Albert,
'it's a short hard fall from the top
of the wash-house step,
so mind you never take it in the dark
or leap across it like your father did,
god rest his soul, carrying two chickens
and not thinking where his foot would fall.'

III

I said to myself: Darwin, one day
these people will understand where you're coming from.
They may not know where you're headed
but they'll get the gist of it.
Just put that slim blue flower behind your ear again
and sing those gentle songs of love:
the rushed-heart, the red-twist of a salmon jumping.
Who wants to hear about violence
when you can see that down the High Street
or in your living room, where you rise like the walking dead
and with that sleep-face white-torn look
admit to being no good in bed to your woman,
who is busy training your canary
to perform fellatio? But this is the Nineties.
There are machines for that now.

Darwin, let's face it –
out under the cold bright look of the stars
we are no nearer Nirvana.
The best we can do is smoke blow
and drink a little whisky on the side.
These words are only words.
They don't pay bills.
They don't make love for us,
like canaries can.
But if they act as a pause
between sleeping and waking,
if they wind firmly like a red thread
between your fingers, moving
and unmoving, and like that ancient
warning they are not heeded,
then you can sow that seed
in the deep sleep of innocence
and hush your woman's mouth
with it before morning.

Loco

There is a train,
an endless track of railroad in my head.

The tracks are over-run with seed,
they clamour with the scent of grass.

Beneath the bridge,
an arch of moss has taken hold.

The flags are up.
The whistle blows – 3.30 every day

a ritual of steam and speed
and racing wind.

I fashioned you from singing-steel.
I hammered out a ring

that cooled in locomotive style.
I took your breath,

your cold indifference
and blew it through a tunnel

like an iron god –
the shriek, the whistle in the dark!

I am all talk,
all track.

I sway as grass
green-bent on gravel in the heat,

the fire of your passing,
steam-blown-white, unstoppable.

Green Waters

Like a fox with the dogs after me
          up to my thighs in the feverish reeds
I wade into green waters
          strip down to tits   belly-flop into the flow
You were in my dreams last night
          less what you said   more how you filled me
And this morning   this morning
          how do you say   *dipsomaniac*

A bead of sweat on the back of a bull
          The voicelessness of sex
No longer any boundaries to breach
          flooding me   a bitch on heat
Translating free-hand into form
          my sheets are wet   green waters
You bark   I get the fierce desire
          to rush ahead   the order to remain

Love Me Not

You love me,
you love me not.
I am a dandelion clock.

You blow my swift drift
like a week's wages at the races.

When did the green stalk
come to a head?
I must have missed it
in the rush
and race of living.

Heavy with seeds,
I am a pomegranate.
Take me
and eat me;

don't worry,
you will only be here
for a season.

Gather me in great armfuls –

ivy, holly, mistletoe,
the church will have to close its doors –

bury me
beneath the altar-piece:
unseen, ritualistic, pagan.

I keep a stone
under my pillow.
The moon will have it.

Last Letter from Paris

This looks more like Japanese,
like the contents of a matchbox
scattered higgledy-piggledy
over the thin white sheet,
your name somewhere among all this
graffiti, an initial, a pictograph,
a bold line.

But in between the tiny stick-insect letters,
the tall thin women
Modigliani probably knew,
I spot a word,
accurate, definable,

surrounded by a half-deciphered telegram
pitted with stops like a strawberry,
a communication best taken *au nature*,
sans comma, *sans* consonant,
but leaning into italics
like a man into a high wind.

Horoscope Dancing

You will not cross into that smoky room.
There was a time – but now it's passed.

Your feet are dancing to a different tune.
We touch, but only while the music lasts,

and when I talk you through your chart,
the music says far more than words could do.

Like stars, we are a million years apart,
though every angle in between is true.

That smoke-filled room where we have met
a thousand times is just my empty heart.

Your *je ne sais quoi*, our *tête à tête*,
were simply ways to set the record straight.

You've moved away, and I've moved on,
so why am I still dancing to your Moon?

Brighton Pilgrimage

She drives down through the dawn:
Brighton streets, traffic-lights, railings,
the Indian summer of the Pavilion,
white-washed terraced houses,
green lawns dotted with sprinklers,
surrounded by wallflowers, roses.
A lone police patrol-car on its beat.

Coming out onto the promenade,
sea becomes a flicker in the mirror,
a long incessant flash of silver
at her shoulder, indicating left
and casting off along the coast.
Not stopping to read the signs,
the place-names, green arrows,

but following the drift of the wind,
due west. She adjusts the mirror;
fumbles, eyes straight ahead, for
her sunglasses on the dashboard.
It was like a dream she once had,
a landscape of the mind, useless
as a now unbeaten track, stopped

like a clock, tickless, unchiming,
not even the second hand moving.
She has driven all night. It is
morning, late spring or summer,
birds drifting out over driftwood
on the long line of the beach,
a man in shirt-sleeves, staring.

The end of the promenade is
a safety-marker, warning-buoy.
Then a cafe, open for business –
a woman out on the step, sweeping.
The sign says: 'All Day Breakfast'.
Two black dogs lie at the roadside
like strange bookends, motionless.

This is the place it started from:
an oak tree root, it winds out
from its origins like a snake,
moving in all directions at once.
She cannot resist, cannot stop.
She is the figure on the beach,
too distant to contact, a dot

halfway between the tidewall
and the tide. The water turns.
It does not have the indolence
of stars, the sophistication
of a satellite in sling-shot orbit,
but in the shallows, the slow
brackish water of the rockpool,

it is the enemy of time, still
unchanged, forever turning.
This mirrored millpond sea,
this copper-coloured coast,
the strangle-hold of estuary,
have stood stock still for years
in ebb and flow monotony.

The villages have grown to towns
of course, with schools, shops,
penny arcades, the sprawl
of make-shift modern bungalows.
But not this view, the estuary
pulled into rhythm by the sea –
nothing here has changed.

Deserted factories, each window
broken by a different stone
along the jagged water's edge.
House-boats moored uneasily,
up to their shoulders in silt,
their painted timbers peeling
from the frame, water-logged.

No other sign of life,
no welcome for a woman
who takes that winding road
along the waterside, looks
out to sea and sees herself
beside an ancient traffic-light
still turning green to red,

stopping an invisible flow
of traffic from the right.
She waits, conditioned to
instruction without cause.
This peace, this timeless blue,
evaded her for thirty years
like sleep; its dark circles

are bruising her eyes.
She wants to stop the car
beside the blanket of the sea,
walk into its white folds
like a child, but the lights
ahead are turning green;
she keeps on driving.

This is the picket fence,
the gate, the garden wall,
a small green square of lawn
where she bent her head
back in the lap of the daisies,
first looked up at the sun
and was made fierce by it.

Like a tall ship in a bottle,
she had to learn to fold herself
into the rigid glass of home,
although the sea had always
beckoned, running beside her
like a shadow on water,
ship-thrown, spray-blown.

Here in this narrow street,
she first perfected cuckoo-
calls, dubbed the briar patch
the wild dog-rose and called
herself by different names –
but none would ever fit
until she found her own.

With the engine running,
she sits, watches the curtain
twitch, lets the sun bounce
back off the dark windows.
She wakes, shakes herself
like a dog out of water,
and fumbles for first gear.

She turns and takes the inland
road. Where does the line
begin, drawn through the time
of the journey, the stopping-in,
the moving-out, the destination?
In the slant of her rear-view mirror,
the sea always a blur, beginning.

Post-Sirenists

We're coming out like moles
at the end of a dark tunnel,

edging, noses to the light,
whiskers flaring.

Their dirt is on our paws,
flaking with each shove towards the sky.

Mama Vole, Papa Badger:
a snapshot of burrowing.

Beneath the earth, safe from the shells,
the stench of fear,

we're coming up for air, too ashamed to hear
the silence and relief of their all-clear.

Wee Sleekit Tim'rous Beastie

(for Judy and David)

Your husband is reciting Burns at dinner
but you're paying, so I watch the flicker

of the candle as we listen, broad Scots
against the kitchen clattering of pots.

When he goes back to get my books,
I follow him through snowy streets.

Each car has tracked a different path:
erratic forklines on a tablecloth.

The train is late again: a midnight ride
that takes me through the countryside

at speed, the ugly woman opposite
is reading someone else's glossy mag.

The stations flicker past, a cold blue
phasing out an orange sky, neon glow

of city lights caught in her windowframe,
pulsing now with unexpected rain.

I hear his voice above the clicker-clack
and change of track, backing in the dark

to Euston's slick efficiency, *sotto voce:*
I wad be laith to rin an' chase thee.

Across the candle-flame, he hands
a well-thumbed page of Robbie Burns.

The Translator

La fraîcheur du matin peint
la vitre, une main qui bouge,
rebouge, y met des couleurs de palette
comme un œil qui regarde sans clignotant
un jardin sans oiseaux.

The freshness of the morning paints
the glass like a hand which moves,
moves again, puts on the colours
of a palette – an eye watching
a birdless garden, unblinking.

The morning freshness paints
the window as a hand must move,
move on, placing palette colours
like a wide eye, looking
across a garden without birds.

The pane is painted fresh
as morning colours, hand-like
moving, motionless, replacing
paint as if it were an open eye,
an empty garden, soundless.

Fresh as garden colours, morning
on the winking window-pane
becomes a painter
waiting for the eyeless birds
which never come.

The birds no longer fly
where paint is like a lidless eye
against the backdrop of the glass:
these freshened colours hand
the morning to the moving sky.

Misreading the Classics

I *The Master Builder*
(for Virgil)

First, he learns how to build
with the crook of the sun in his eyes,
a cool wind at his back.

His is the voice
of the hive-maker, the worker bee,
self-generating, cell by cell into the future.

Second, his task
involves a steady hand –
threading beads, buttercups, camels.

There is no room
for impatience.
Immortality takes forever.

Third, he must be strong enough
to give the *coup de grâce*
or leave demands that it be done:

each block must be carved out by hand;
each stress requires a counterstress;
each weight must balance out the plan.

Last, his aim will be
to stand clear of the shadows
of the past

not watch the prows
of distant ships,
but reach beyond, build high, surpass.

II *Sonnet*
(*for John Keats*)

My most perfect man, chevalier,
doomed early on to die abroad, alone,
hanging by a word to every painful day
or just two words: *success* and then *forlorn*.
What whipped your entrails out, was it desire,
this gnawing sense of having failed some test,
or were you truly touched with Homer's fire
and dared not live too long after his kiss?
What made your soul was not that fleeting song
you heard, or half-heard as someone else
once said, but that you got it wrong, half-wrong –
and that, as Frost said, made the difference.
You had more courage than I think you knew;
this hand is warm, that water always blue.

III *The Weaver Worker*
(*for Gerard Manley Hopkins*)

So-fervent, flecked with fear of failure, ridi-
cule, you split infinitives to (how strange!) ask the
roar, the ringing sea: sky-scared as Pliny
in the face of, glory of godhead, the master!

You dart, depart from word to flashing word;
exhilarate the pace: the word paced-forth,
fear-damned – a second Dante – darkness-dared
but hungered for, hung-on, flushed with its force,
you walk the foam, the freedom of voice found;
ecstatic-astride the circling blue, heavens' skies.

Where are you eddies now, your flow, flown down?
Taken, flying the storm as a lightning-dart flies,
piece-piercing and threading, treading down, ah,
how each word works, defies its definition, past.

IV *Headstone*
(for W.B. Yeats)

What could divide that country from this man
or take a cold star from a tower's height,
when every word recalls the fiercest tongue,
the strongest love unloved, the clearest sight?
The stream runs on, the birth of something strange
takes place beneath a dying monument:
all heads turn west to see the restless change
from fire to fire, from voice to voiced intent.

The wind is peeling stone from silent stone,
revealing bones the colour of a woman's hair:
ambiguous, uncompromising, stern.
All that it takes is taken from in here.
Some prophecy of unrequited love
has shaken lives before and shakes them still,
a taste of how it feels to feel the rough
confines of death and bend them to your will.

Having read up on the subject

this is a straight-forward choice between
understanding and misunderstanding.
Not just for me, watching the thin line of the road
snake off into the distance under a sky
that could have been purple a minute ago

but is reaching a dull red as it sinks into shadow,
but for these also, letting the thin line of the print
take off into the distance under a sky
that has expunged every last drop of light now
like a wiped-down blackboard

at the end of a curiously long classroom.
But what does it matter how much it weighs
unless this is a barter-system, so that
each word like each tall strand of wheat
is exchanged for lunch under a hot sun, a grape-hung

patio poised high above a breath-taking view
at Les Baux de Provence for example
where the wind spits dirt in your eye
unless you shelter in the narrow doorways
or dart sideways down those long cool passages

to sun-struck terracotta, a veranda wasped
with honeysuckle, where *petites baguettes*
pile up in baskets by the door.
This then is where it ultimately leads:
not to some classic moment of inspiration –

ahhh! the light-bulb caught above your head –
but here, now, drinking wine with some friends
or dining alone above the white rocks at Les Baux,
knowing that soon it will be time for the long drive home,
the giving and receiving of keys,

the letters piled up in the porch, even the click
of the ansaphone signalling nothing
so that this minute, this hour, is somehow special:
worth remembering, taking apart later
like an airfix model, only to put it back

into its composite parts, or like bones, broken
but meticulously reset as they are rested.
There will come a time when even this is finished:
when there are no more bones to set
and that afternoon on the veranda

is nothing but a memory, a word
that someone read somewhere,
caught up, nodding but disorientated,
as one who having stumbled on a secret place
discovers they were not the first to have found it.

Bonfire

There's no room in that circle
for an outer ring of darkness
where the cupped hand
catches a spark,

though a whisper might
crackle into obscurity
like smoke on the rise.
In the lucidity of exile

these faces blur to a word
too dark to read –
foreign, dissolving,
unpronounceable,

based on an alphabet
of the invisible.
But to the one at the back
it is a single burning line,

cool and clear
as the end of a dream,
unequivocably
not sleeping but waking.

Century of Rain

Out on the tarmac,
under the black houses,
I hear them – voices

voices, muttering
old women.
The rain brings down

new scales
while I am walking, shedding
light and sharp,

the silver skin of a snake,
replacing.
The gutter takes

my cast-offs,
but the houses are still muttering
through blacked-out windows.

Is it wrong to desire
a voice original as sin,
not to shuffle wet-bellied through the shite

of a whole century of rain?
They cling
like insects to my skin:

I am dark with them.
A storm-cloud,
a plague of locusts coming down –

the air is alive! –
replacing my skin with their own,
mute chameleon.

Wavelength

I build the perfect silence with my hands:
a pyramid of sorts, an arch, the gaping
mouth of Agamemnon's beehive tomb.

When all is said and done, what will remain
but silence? I've lost the will to speak,
but send my empty hands to seek new land.

They will come back. Will they come back?
Distilling words until no words are left
becomes a concentration of the mind,

an endless search for essences of sound:
the slack white sands, the echo of the hills:
will they come back? They will come back.

You'll know the perfect silence when it comes.
It has the outward look of architecture
(structured stress), the inward hum of bees.

It stands alone, discarding time as one
who, trusting, shrugs a raincoat to the ground
before the storm is through. No reckless jump

from words to space, but something planned,
a leap of faith, inevitable to those
who welcome it into their silent band.

Head for Heights

Don't tell me how, just ask me when.
I wasn't born with two mouths for nothing.

These lips have crossed a thousand legs
in prayer and dream and idle play.

You cannot blame a compass for its pull
nor break the Poles apart by melting ice

into a glass and telling me to chill:
I'm tenser than an arrow in mid-flight.

What shall I see when swinging low
above the earth's blue line and into time

no one has trekked across or catalogued
or skidded on or glided through?

Will I retell the building, line by line,
blue by blue, of a horizon in progress?

Or will I be grabbing at the parachute,
jerking the long cord but still falling?

Who handed out the dud to me? I would be
silk and fire across the surface of a lake,

the trace of an old wound on my lips
like salt blooms on the skin of a sailor

if they let me. And how free-fall
when the role-call is predestined?

The phony accents, the false beards
are risible. We take no risks

without permission. Our only hope
lies in making the invisible visible.

Original Skin

I walk out into the water,
welcome it:
this blue mouth
opening
in an exquisite yawn.

The tiny shoals of fish
are teeth. The rush
and roll of no-tide tide
moves over me
in waves. To hang

by the breadth of a hair
at the height of a curl,
is to float shallow
belly-up
into the curve.

Their net is cast
too wide, pulled tight
into a stranglehold:
one fish caught as
swiftly as the next.

I am a flounder,
splashing soundless
under a blunt sickle.
Tonight, I will be
bouillabaisse

or *hollandaise*,
some café off the quay
in Old Marseille,
renamed
la pièce de resistance.

The sea will be
a memory:
where they shed my skin,
a taste of something
less ephemeral.

The Gift

And the emptiness,
never forget the emptiness.

Did you expect a gift,
free-gratis, unacknowledged, to be fun?

A bag of tricks
for when you're out of lies?

There are no rules
to make you feel secure, no rules.

But what there is,
there is the sun. It

shoots through you like a bullet in the neck,
a flash of green, a field alight.

That spinning when you were a child:
eyes closed, arms spread.

The whole world there
but in your head, unassailable.

Aphrodite Revisited

When I say *I love you*
it means I love you and not
I need you or *this is the way*
things will be and don't argue.

When we took that walk
by the disused canal
and I stood by the lilies
in a white glow of fusion,

were you slave or lover,
or was the prospect too daunting?

Forgetting to Remember

(for Christiana Evelyn Beatrice Holland, 1903-1997)

You turned your face to the wall a year ago,
waiting for this. Not a word, not a whisper
passed your lips. In your eyes, not a flicker
when they came and went, those ghosts
dressed like your children but unknown, older.
And your son was not your husband, although
you must have thought so, trying his name.

The nurse came by, with something
to help you sleep, but you didn't. Sat there
as though for a portrait, erasing the canvas
with cataracts, your glasses deep bottle-green.
A few years shy of the century, you were still
in that sunny front room in Maison Dieu,
preparing to paint, though they'd sold it
to pay the home fees ten years before.

I was almost as tall as you at eleven,
sunlight glinting off that shade you wore,
one eye patched like a pirate's.
And after the guns at Arromanches,
he could never hear the racing results
so you had to repeat, repeat yourself
until he was gone, memory evaporating
then, too swiftly, like turps you'd left in the sun.

Canzoni

Your image blurs
in a fingerprint of rain,

shark's-eye twitching the lens
like a landed fish
as you gather yourself.

This is your funeral.
You cannot afford to be absent.

                    *

Where the world was, there is a hole.
At the bottom, a rotten box
opens steel hinges.

The church stiffens
into the future, beckoning.

The goddess bends over the pram
in a wave of bright light and eucalyptus.
Her skin has the look of scouring pads.
She is angry, then diffident.

When she goes,
she leaves something with me –
so tiny I could tuck it under my fingernail
and not notice –
but it shines, it sparkles!

It turns in the wind like a seed
hungry for soil, then sits all summer
under the red bell of the rhubarb.

I hear it pressing
cool dark clay
with its arm stumps.

*

This coal bunker is so drab
it is almost innocuous:

inhabiting the air like a virus,
its unseen spores drift inwards.

This photograph
must have been taken in '68 –

he came out with a sledgehammer
not long after

and reduced it to rubble –
but I remember the smell, the gritty feel of it.

Coal dust is like pollen –
I carried it around in my lungs

summer after summer,
a black hive.

*

It was always raining
and the bookcase was always full.

After the rug ended,
before the skirting board began,

your dark spine shone like skin
under my fingers.

You were a shadow
on an x-ray,
growing and deforming.

They should have had you removed

but you were part of me –
a sucker, coming out of the soil
where the graft root was accidentally buried.

Your words hatch
white clutch-eggs in my larynx
twenty years on,

where the dull sheen of pearls
first gleamed under my palate.

*

This is no mosquito.
The lump is already swelling and purpling
like the eyesockets of an aborted head.

It stinks of old cats, fishbones, dustbin lids.

It has no name,
so reluctantly I give it yours –
unwanted, it's been skulking about for years
and demands purpose.

I will give birth to a wolf bite.

*

The car ticks over,
the soft green *pit pit pit*
of rain on the windscreen.

It is three minutes to twelve.

When the lightning comes,
it is a steel pin
in the throat of the morning,

holding noon from midnight
and one swift breath
from the other.

Afterwards, I shudder down the lane
like an old woman,

thirty seconds closer
to whatever took you.

                    *

This is not *The Purple Rose of Cairo*
where you will walk out of the screen,
a *dea ex machina*,

but the echo of an echo,
repeating myself
as I try to unwrangle

future from present,
present from past historic,

finding them all
on the same skein of wool
like runners from a strawberry,
budding intermittently.

There will be no
ice cream at the interval.

Down, down, the house lights
have all gone down,

leaving nothing but the waiting,
as I step outside my own skin

into the silver skin of history.

*

This room breathes
the dark stench of the Inquisition.
She does not have the answers to your questions.

Will you stretch her on the rack?
Is she your next victim?

A star swivels
above the one glinting eye
of the brickwork, aching
to be opened and examined.

Milk-white, it tenses and folds.
She is not a cat. She will not drink it.
It stands for insanity, knowledge.

Your questions beat about her head
like sisters, their blood is on her fingers.

*

God, for a heart rent like a veil –

flayed on an anvil
like the skin of a walrus –

ripped, beaten so thin
its veins, its valves,
the bright gush of aorta,
wither to sun-dried red chillis.

*

Her black-hole-eye collapses
in on itself. The debris

thickens and follows.

Tell me, old man,
what was it like
to sleep with the goddess,

to taste her death,
the retreat of it?

Your mind is a morgue.

Images lie tagged on the tables,
smiling postmortem,
the flash of a shutter.

For this sad pilgrimage to end,
the beast herself

must rise and walk,
bearing her slab
like a standard before her.

*

There is a bullet
lodged in your gullet,

a small shining oblong
with the voice
and cry of a woman.

The hare, the grouse,
the blood-flecked rabbit,
dance on your rain gibbet,
creaking their shut eyes.

The sea walks tall
in the distance,
a whisper of silver
past the high grasses

where the moon hangs
like a crude symbol
over a rough cot.

There is no way
to ward off this evil.

You will lie face-down
for centuries,
picking out her features:
stones from mud.

*

I step back,
listening to where the ripples
found me,

the still drop of a stone
into dark water,
the endless concentric circles.

After the stone's entry,
the waters heal themselves
like lips closing on silence.

From the depths,
the world comes back
as a blue shadow,

seen through the shallow eye
of a stone.

*

Worm wriggles
inside his fur pouch, stretching.

The animal died last month.

His mouth is squeaking
the tin whistle
of its teeth, restlessly.

Then the wind shifts.
His damp striations rise
and coil.

Someone has hung someone else
out to dry.

*

The clock calls in the hall
with its first hand, striking.

She says something,
but the crack of your heart
is too loud to hear it.

Through the dark room,
you see the glint of her breath
as she turns into the pillow.

She knows. She knows.

The sheets pull like dust-jackets
into your hand.

*

Harnessed to the air,
she is anathema –

no birds touch her.

The stinging flail
of the sun catches her ankle.

She is anchored
to a heat-source, incandescent.

Her marigold mouth
blisters
and shrivels –

is this how death feels? –

her hair withers
like a field of burnt bracken.

The thrush
starts from the thicket
as she arches, hollow candle,
from one form to another.

The lawn leaves a charred circle
where her feet fall.

*

Black ash
under the broad sweep of an oak.

Starlings sift
through its fingers.

She imagined herself violent,
failing to see how the line breaks
at the meridian,

leaving her stranded, unalterable.

Too far inland for the sea,
crashing between houses, gleaming
like the blunt edge of a sickle –

where a boat might cross and recross,
telling its history –

but still now as the centre,
silent, irreproachable.

Song for the Living

The whole thing comes together
like a broken jar before the act of displacement.
It's a tugging, a bird pulling a worm from the wet earth,

the tide sludging back into a deserted harbour,
muffled bells calling the faithful to worship.
It has nothing to do with idealism, merely necessity

and the dull tread of routine.
How the muscle flexes as the axis rotates,
taking foot, wrist, ankle through a narrow doorway.

Contracting with sunlight, this aperture
squeezes mechanically to a pinprick:
something leaps neatly, avoiding the synapse.

Timing is everything, coming in through the blue valve,
pumping out through the red valve, wave upon wave
in this restless arrestless motion, so that to break step

is to break rhythm.
To break rhythm is to move outside time.
No mis-step

but a calculated risk.
What is there, in the heart,
before the blood starts pumping?

This cannot last forever. The circles diminish
little by little, just as the echoes fade out
under a railway bridge in the coming dusk.

They cannot move onward and outward
for everything is dying, stripping itself down,
edging forwards into the darkness

with an unknown, unreasonable, propulsion.
Lift the bulbs: dry and separate them.
The autumn garden needs no explanation.

The sun goes behind a cloud,
or a cloud moves across the sun.
Significance in the fall of a sparrow.

A catalyst is always something larger than ourselves,
not necessarily better
but capable of being hooked onto.

The sound of her footsteps in the passage
is endlessly alluring because unseen,
part of that intractable pull of the unattainable.

Where does the power come from,
forcing the bulbhead into flower?
Millipedes crawl through its root span

like children, transforming.
The implacable earth covers them.
It will always be night,

for once light comes
there will be no turning back,
though some might call that redemption.

Pausing for breath, as a woman who has
climbed seven hills,
can see the seven she has yet to climb:

an invisible thread, caught on her sleeve,
is slowly, inexorably, unravelling.
That chaos is inherent, breaks all bonds.

No, not chaos, but decay,
a candle burning at the other end of light,
the counterbalance and the weight.

The word takes shape within itself, uncoiling
like the earthworm from the earth, blind
but sensing endless healing.

An empty market-place, the village square
peopled with shadows, and the old church
leaning against the elm in an attitude of dismay.

Here, the live bird mocks the drifters,
tourists in the wrong town, early closing
and all the pubs shut up for the holiday.

There will be no bargaining, only
a straight exchange under the town hoardings.
These bells, caught on the air like a child's kite

biting and eddying with the flow
are no less real because imagined.
The shopkeepers shut their shops,

follow each other to the village green
where there will be dancing and juggling
and the round ringing bowl of the storyteller,

the maypole and the may tree,
the ribbons and the dancers, the crowd
and the sweat of the daisies.

Can I empty my mind as it ought to be emptied?
Not leave one trace behind for the sunlight,
caught between the apple tree

and the tennis court in a pocket of light?
Here, away from the people and the dancing,
stone breathes like a woman asleep in an orchard,

playing the green dapple against closed lids,
keeping the wall firm, the step trembling,
the narrow path alive with bees.

To be emptied implies capacity,
an earlier saturation drained out slowly
into the cracks of a baked earth,

a ceremony of generosity, transferring fullness
from one medium to another,
just as the act of emptiness implies vacuum,

a transitional state demanding repletion.
The bumblebee waddles
from one sticky fascination to another, humming.

All desire comes from the voice of survival:
the stone, aware of each pressure,
the tree, the dry earth, the sun

revolving patiently as the others revolve patiently,
the air quivering, compact: 'Signify.
Preserve evidence for the tide has no memory.'

Two steps into the house, the stone ship, afloat
on this silent morning like the *Marie Celeste*,
empty, unexplained except for a shriek of laughter

from the tennis court over the high box-hedge.
Emptiness, where a volley might come
unexpectedly from the sidelines.

The connection between time and place
may be part of that memory,
but only part

for its scent mixes
unruly with the others,
brushing against ankles in a wave of release.

This could be the station
where a train passes
without stopping,

glimpsed for a moment
through a tunnel of speed
before vanishing into its own echo.

A prophecy of self-prophecy, changeless
as the Mediterranean, constantly
failing to advance.

The struggle to have purpose
is the struggle of the fruit tree
to bear fruit.

At every turn, we touch the intangible
without knowing it, and without knowing,
it becomes our foundation, our keystone.

Conservatory windows reveal a gravelled path,
a wooden bench, where cigarette stubs
in the flower-beds mark the passage of time.

It is not enough
to be aware of its passing,
for that awareness lasts only a lifetime.

Act now, the azaleas say,
bursting their red petals,
act now in glorious futility.

Song for the Dying

This is a history of mismanagement,
meaning absence of order
and order of absence. Out of the blank night,

a lyre-player tunes herself to the rocks
as the goddess sings – naked
but for the wild blossom tangling their hair.

Where is the word born that comes under the stars
in the tense heat of summer?
Here, at the water's edge, an olive tree reflects

itself, emblem of the breath
that fills the gap after the dark exhales.
Pliant, the womb first swells and then dilates,

exuding emptiness after repletion. A snake
slips out of that dark mouth like retribution.
The song which sings itself is not a song

of the censored, but of the uncensorable:
a mass of white light
into which motion proceeds, unflinching.

The 'I' who might have spoken without thinking
now thinks without speaking
but the voiceless can be, should be, heard.

What is one life worth if not everything?
This urge, trodden inwards like a grape,
breaks free of its restraints.

The purple fabric splits and splitting
makes a thousand threads of light:
now unconnected, now the same.

All sounds reverberate and stir the bell.
The fall devours, recurs as tree by tree
unfold their dying leaves. Mosaic-crossed,

the mirrored pieces face a chequered board:
fall, fighting, as the heart must fall
and falter on at the silent centre.

If the word is death, why lust after it
unless death is the word inverted, unspoken?
(Spoken, it shatters the wheel, turning.)

This wave demands no stop nor fierce internal force
if pushed on by the word, explosive sound, unreasoning.
To take it out of time is to transplant the thought,

endemic in the mind, of wave and fire and stone.
A mechanism winds by hand, requiring hands
and voice, command. There is no pleasure

in the purely wrought, the artificial bird.
If song is worth the song alone,
there is no merit in the descant, echo taking,

breaking from its score like a tree
outgrowing its support, following without question
its natural course, as each soil breeds its image.

So darkness sings only of darkness, and light
of the light, unregarding – taking a flight of stairs
to a small dark flat, winter and the pipes

all burst with the cold, one window open
and the dawn bringing a stiff body homewards.
It must have been fate or luck which

intervened, turning light to darkness –
the ultimate act.
This poisoned honey seeps from every pore.

It is a pact, unspoken, a hushed
conspiracy of the given, a path only
for the broken, not the whole, the chosen.

The last act of dying is the ceremony of living:
here, where the descent into flame
is not pursuit of death but of love,

some foreign coin is rattling the till.
Even for the ignorant, the wordless,
the currency of death is knowledge.

Books lie open on the desk, indecipherable,
unnerving: row upon row of cold clear figures,
lines flowing but not touching,

describing the house but not entering.
Nothing to be done but the crossing:
a still moon drifting dark water,

one muttered word, the exchange of a token,
and the graceless past, such passive grace,
takes all accounts, enumerates.

Unalterable, the song deceives.
Sing on, for the unalterable is everything.
The kiss betrays, the voice denies.
All stones ring with the hammer, the forging.